TABLE OF CONTENTS

Introduction

My story begins seven years ago at almost 60 lbs. I was on a mission to transform my body into something healthier. I was introduced to many new diets and exercise programs, some of which failed to achieve any significant results, and others made a small contribution to my weight loss. The internet is full of amazing diets that promise to help me lose a lot of weight with little effort, but fail to deliver. Nothing came close to achieving my weight loss goal. Then I discovered the Lean and Green diet. I was thrilled with the supplies I received for the plan I chose, but the Lean and Green meals are proving to be a tough nut to crack because I don't know what to prepare that meets the diet's recommendations.

I wish I could take the guesswork out of the whole process to focus on taking the portions of food provided and not spend too much time following the nutritional information. However, with the guidance of my dietitian, I was able to combine some vegetable recipes to make a healthy diet. Despite this, the process was nerve-wracking. I documented the recipes and diets, followed the diet strictly and experienced excellent results. I lost weight beyond my expectations and developed a new relationship with food. Six years later, I am still active, strong and maintaining a healthy weight. Eating Lean & Green has become part of my lifestyle, and I have documented my Lean and Green diet in this cookbook to help you make a healthy choice with your diet .
I have struggled with an unhealthy body weight for most of my life, the inspiration to write this diet book comes from a deep desire to help others on a similar journey. I'm excited to share nutritious and healthy Lean and Green diets that are also incredibly satisfying and delicious.As you know, the Lean and Green diet is a commercial diet, but it is considered one of the most popular diets that have brought many

benefits over the three decades. Lean and Green is a home cooked meal option that encourages weight loss through strict homemade green recipes to improve blood lipids, sugar levels and better overall health. Lean and Green is an easy, affordable, and long-lasting diet to lose weight quickly and effectively. This book will be your guide so that you can enjoy delicious and healthy food that can improve your health.

Are you tired of diets that promise results but take a huge amount of time and effort to plan? Or are you looking for a diet that will help you lose unnecessary weight in a fast, safe and convenient way? You can finally stop agonizing over losing time, money or inspiration with this Lean and Green cookbook. The recipes in this book will help you lose weight in the shortest possible time, and will also boost your confidence and promote motivation to continue.

The recipes contain ingredients that will help you lose weight and maintain good overall health without worrying about regaining the weight in the future.

This book helps you develop a healthy relationship with food while educating you with the health benefits and nutritional information in each of the recipes.

Soon, preparing a healthy diet will be a breeze, as you now have the information on how to prepare meals that fit your needs.

CHAPTER 1

BREAKFAST RECIPES

1. <u>Chia Seed Gel with Pomegranate and Nuts</u>

Prep Time: 5 mins

Cook Time: 10 mins

Servings: 3

<u>*Ingredients*</u>:

- 20 g hazelnuts

- 20 g walnuts

- 120 ml almond milk

- 4 tbsp chia seeds

- 4 tbsp pomegranate seeds

- 1 teaspoon agave syrup

- Some lime juices

<u>*Directions*</u>:

1. Finely chop the nuts.

2. Mix the almond milk with the chia seeds.

3. Let everything soak for 10 to 20 minutes.

4. Occasionally stir the mixture with the chia seeds.

5. Stir in the agave syrup.

6. Pour 2 tablespoons of each mixture into a dessert glass.

7. Layer the chopped nuts on top.

8. Cover the nuts with 1 tablespoon each of the chia mass.

9. Sprinkle the pomegranate seeds on top and serve everything.

Nutrition:

- kcal: 238 g

- Carbohydrates: 8 g

- Protein: 2 g

- Fat: 21 g

2. Smoothie Bowl with Spinach, Mango and Muesli

Prep Time: 8 mins

Cook Time: 0 mins

Servings: 1

Ingredients:

- 150g yogurt

- 30g apple

- 30g mango

- 30g low carb muesli

- 10g spinach

- 10g chia seeds

Directions:

1. Soak the spinach leaves and let them drain.

2. Peel the mango and cut it into strips.

3. Remove apple core and cut it into pieces.

4. Put everything except the mango together with the yogurt in a blender and make a fine puree out of it.

5. Put the spinach smoothie in a bowl.

6. Add the muesli, chia seeds, and mango.

7. Serve the whole thing

Nutrition:

- kcal: 261 g

- Carbohydrates: 20 g

- Protein: 12 g

- Fat: 20 g

3. <u>Millet Porridge</u>

Prep Time: 5 mins

Cook Time: 20 mins

Servings: 2

<u>*Ingredients*</u>:

- Sea salt

- 1 tbsp. finely chopped coconuts

- 1/2 cup unsweetened coconut milk

- 1/2 cup rinsed and drained millet

- 1-1/2 cups alkaline water

- 3 drops liquid stevia

<u>*Directions*</u>:

1. Sauté the millet in a non-stick skillet for about 3 minutes.

2. Add salt and water then stir.

3. Let the meal boil then reduce the amount of heat.

4. Cook for 15 minutes then add the remaining ingredients.

   Stir.

5. Cook the meal for 4 extra minutes.

6. Serve the meal with toping of the chopped nuts.

Nutrition:

- kcal: 209 g

- Carbohydrates: 37.6 g

- Protein: 7.5 g

- Fat: 4.6 g

4. Pumpkin Spice Quinoa

Prep Time: 10 mins

Cook Time: 0 mins

Servings: 2

Ingredients:

- 1 cup cooked quinoa

- 1 cup unsweetened coconut milk

- 1 large mashed banana

- 1/4 cup pumpkin puree

- 1 tsp. pumpkin spice

- 2 tsps. chia seeds

Directions:

1. In a container, mix all the ingredients.

2. Seal the lid then shake the container properly to mix.

3. Refrigerate overnight.

4. Serve.

Nutrition:

- kcal: 238 g

- Carbohydrates: 8 g

- Protein: 2 g

- Fat: 21 g

5. Zucchini Pancakes

Prep Time: 15 mins

Cook Time: 8 mins

Servings: 8

Ingredients:

- 12 tbsps. alkaline water
- 6 large grated zucchinis
- Sea salt
- 4 tbsps. ground Flax Seeds
- 2 tsps. olive oil   2 finely chopped jalapeño peppers
- 1/2 cup finely chopped scallions

Directions:

1. In a bowl, mix together water and the flax seeds then set it aside.
2. Pour oil in a large non-stick skillet then heat it on medium heat.
3. The add the black pepper, salt, and zucchini.
4. Cook for 3 minutes then transfer the zucchini into a large bowl.
5. Add the flax seed and the scallion's mixture then properly mix it.
6. Preheat a griddle then grease it lightly with the cooking spray.
7. Pour 1/4 of the zucchini mixture into griddle then cook for 3 minutes.

8. Flip the side carefully then cook for 2 more minutes.

9. Repeat the procedure with the remaining mixture in batches. Serve.

Nutrition:

- kcal: 62 g Carbohydrates: 9.6 g Protein: 3.5 g
- Fat: 2.6 g

6. Sweet Cashew Cheese Spread

Prep Time: 5 mins

Cook Time: 5 mins

Servings: 10

Ingredients:

- 5 drops , Stevia

- 2 cups, raw Cashews

- 1/2 cup Water

Directions:

1. Soak the cashews overnight in water.

2. Next, drain the excess water then transfer cashews to a

   food processor.

3. Add in the stevia and the water.

4. Process until smooth.

5. Serve chilled. Enjoy.

Nutrition:

- kcal: 120 g

- Carbohydrates: 5.6 g

- Protein: 3.5 g

- Fat: 8 g

7. Zucchini Breakfast Bars

Prep Time: 10 mins

Cook Time: 35 mins

Servings: 6

Ingredients:

- 1 cup zucchini grated

- ¼ cup coconut butter, softened

- 2 tsp cinnamon

- 1 tbsp chia seeds

- ½ cup hemp hearts

- 2 tbsp granulated erythritol

- A pinch of salt

Directions:

1. Preheat the oven to 375 degrees F.

2. Prepare a baking sheet by lining it with parchment paper.

3. In a large bowl, add the coconut butter, zucchini and erythritol.

4. Add the rest of the ingredients and stir to incorporate . Let the

mixture sit for 5 minutes so that the chia seeds thicken the

batter.

5. Pour the mixture into the prepared pan and smooth the top with

a spatula.

6. Bake for 35 minutes or until the bars are golden brown and firm

to the touch.

7. Allow to cool for at least 30 minutes before removing from oven.

Slice into individual bars and serve.

Nutrition: kcal: 238 g Carbohydrates: 8 g Protein: 2 g Fat: 21 g

8. <u>Bacon Cheeseburger</u>

Prep Time: 5 mins

Cook Time: 15 mins

Servings: 4

<u>Ingredients</u>:

- 1 lb. lean ground beef

- ¼ cup chopped yellow onion

- 1 clove garlic, minced

- 1 Tbsp. yellow mustard

- 1 Tbsp. Worcestershire sauce

- ½ tsp salt

- Cooking spray

- 4 ultra-thin slices cheddar cheese, cut into 6 equal-sized

  rectangular pieces

- 3 pieces of turkey bacon, each cut into 8 evenly-sized rectangular

  pieces

- 24 dill pickle chips

- 4-6 green leaf

- lettuce leaves, torn into 24 small square-shaped pieces

- 12 cherry tomatoes, sliced in half

Directions:

1. Pre-heat oven to 400°F.

2. Combine the garlic, salt, onion, Worcestershire sauce, and beef

   in a medium-sized bowl, and mix well.

3. Form mixture into 24 small meatballs. Put meatballs onto a foil-

   lined baking sheet and cook for 12-15 minutes. Leave oven on.

4. Top every meatball with a piece of cheese, then go back to the

   oven till cheese melts, about 2 to 3 minutes. Let meatballs cool.

5. To assemble bites: on a toothpick layer a cheese-covered meatball, piece of bacon, piece of lettuce, pickle chip, and a tomato half.

Nutrition:

- kcal: 235 g

- Carbohydrates: 11 g

- Protein: 21 g

- Fat: 3 g

9. Baked Breakfast Frittata

Prep Time: 10 mins

Cook Time: 35 mins

Servings: 6

Ingredients:

- 12 eggs

- 1 tsp garlic powder

- 2-1/2 cups mushrooms, chopped

- 1 cup cheddar cheese, shredded

- 1 red bell pepper, chopped

- 1 small onion, chopped

- 1 cup ham, chopped

- 1-1/2 cups asparagus, chopped

- Pepper

- Salt

Directions:

1. Preheat the oven to 375 F. Grease 9*13-inch baking pan.

2. Add asparagus, mushrooms, cheese, bell pepper, onion, and ham into the prepared pan.

3. In a bowl, whisk eggs with garlic powder, pepper, and salt.

4. Pour egg mixture over vegetables and stir gently.

5. Bake for 25-35 minutes or until frittata is set.

6. Slice and serve.

Nutrition:

- kcal: 122 g

- Carbohydrates: 3.8 g

- Protein: 11.2 g

- Fat: 8.5 g

CHAPTER 2

LUNCH RECIPES

10.Risotto with Green Beans, Sweet Potatoes, And

Peas

Prep Time: 30 mins

Cook Time: 4 – 5 hours

Servings: 8

Ingredients:

- 1 large sweet potato, peeled and chopped

- 1 onion, chopped

- 5 garlic cloves, minced

- 2 cups short-grain brown rice

- 1 teaspoon dried thyme

- leaves

- 7 cups low-sodium vegetable broth

- 2 cups green beans, cut in half crosswise

- 2 cups frozen baby peas

- 3 tablespoons unsalted butter

- ½ cup grated Parmesan cheese

Directions:

1. In a 6-quart slow cooker, mix the sweet potato, onion, garlic, rice, thyme, and broth. Cover and cook on low for 3 to 4 hours, or until the rice is tender.

2. Stir in the green beans and frozen peas. Cover and cook on low for 30 to 40 minutes or until the vegetables are tender.

3. Stir in the butter and cheese. Cover and cook on low for 20 minutes, then stir and serve.

Nutrition:

- Calories: 385 kcal Fat: 10 g Carbs: 50 g

11.Herbed Garlic Black Beans

Prep Time: 10 mins

Cook Time: 7 to 9 hours **Servings**: 4

Ingredients:

- 2 cups dried black beans, rinsed and drained

- 1 onions, chopped 4 garlic cloves, minced

- 3 cups low-sodium vegetable broth

- ½ teaspoon salt

- 1 teaspoon dried basil leaves ½ teaspoon dried thyme leaves

- ½ teaspoon dried oregano leaves

Directions:

1. In a 6-quart slow cooker, mix all the ingredients. Cover and cook on low for 7 to 9 hours, or until the beans have absorbed the liquid and are tender.

2. Remove and discard the bay leaf.

Nutrition:

- Calories: 250 kcal

- Carbs: 48 g

- Protein: 20 g

12. Quinoa with Vegetables

Prep Time: 10 mins

Cook Time: 5 to 6 hours **Servings**: 4

Ingredients:

- 1 cups quinoa, rinsed and drained

- 1 onions, chopped 1 carrots, peeled and sliced

- 1 cup sliced cremini mushrooms

- 2 garlic cloves, minced 2 cups low-sodium vegetable broth ½ teaspoon salt 1 teaspoon dried marjoram leaves

- 1/4 teaspoon freshly ground black pepper

Directions:

1. In a 6-quart slow cooker, mix all of the ingredients. Cover and cook on low for 5 to 6 hours, or until the quinoa and vegetables are tender.

2. Stir the mixture and serve.

Nutrition:

- Calories: 204 kcal

- Fat: 3 g

- Carbs: 33 g

- Protein: 7

13.Keto Zucchini Pizza

Prep Time: 10 mins

Cook Time: 15mins

Servings: 2

Ingredients:

- 1/8 cup spaghetti sauce

- ½ zucchini, cut in circular slices

- ½ cup cream cheese Pepperoni slices, for topping ½ cup mozzarella cheese, shredded.

Directions:

1. Preheat the oven to 350 degrees and grease a baking dish.

2. Arrange the zucchini on the baking dish and layer with spaghetti sauce.

3. Top with pepperoni slices and mozzarella cheese.

4. Transfer the baking dish to the oven and bake for about 15

   minutes.

5. Remove from the oven and serve immediately.

Nutrition:

- Calories: 440 kcal

- Fat: 40 g

- Carbs: 3.8 g

- Protein: 14.8 g

14. Herbed Wild Rice

Prep Time: 10 mins **Cook Time**: 4 to 6 hours **Servings**: 4

Ingredients:

- 2 cups wild rice, rinsed and drained

- 3 cups Roasted Vegetable Broth (here)

- 1 onion, chopped ½ teaspoon salt

- ½ teaspoon dried thyme leaves

- ½ teaspoon dried basil leaves 1 bay leaf

- 1/2 cup chopped fresh flat-leaf parsley

Directions:

1. In a 6-quart slow cooker, mix the wild rice, vegetable broth, onion, salt, thyme, basil, and bay leaf. Cover and cook on low for 4 to 6 hours, or until the wild rice is tender but still firm. You can cook this dish longer until the wild rice pops; that will

take about 7 to 8 hours.

2. Remove and discard the bay leaf.

3. Stir in the parsley and serve.

Nutrition:

- Calories: 258 kcal

- Fat: 6 g

- Carbs: 58 g

- Protein: 6g

15. Delicious Low Carb Chicken Caesar Salad

Prep Time: 15 mins

Cook Time: 6 mins

Servings: 4

Ingredients:

- 1 cup of Parmesan crisps

- 1 head of Romaine lettuce, chopped

- 2 cup of Grape tomatoes, halved

- 2 grilled chicken breasts, sliced

For Keto Caesar Dressing:

- 1/3 cup of Caesar salad dressing

Directions:

1. Chill the Caesar salad dressing in the refrigerator.

2. Combine the grape tomatoes, romaine lettuce, and cooked

chicken.

3. Break the cheese crisps into bits and sprinkle on the salad and

drizzle with the dressing. Mix to combine.

Nutrition: Calories: 400 kcal; Fat: 20 g; Carbs: 8 g ; Protein: 33g

16. Yogurt Garlic Chicken

Prep Time: 30 mins

Cook Time: 60 mins

Servings: 6

Ingredients:

- Pita bread rounds

- halved (6 pieces)

- English cucumber,

- sliced thinly, w/ each slice halved (1 cup)

Chicken & vegetables:

- Olive oil (3 tablespoons)   Black pepper, freshly ground (1/2 teaspoon)

- Chicken thighs, skinless, boneless (20 ounces)

- Bell pepper, red, sliced into half-inch portions (1 piece) Garlic

  cloves, chopped finely (4 pieces)

- Cumin, ground (1/2 teaspoon)

- Red onion, medium, sliced into half-inch wedges (1 piece)

- Yogurt, plain, Fat: free (1/2 cup)

- Lemon juice (2 tablespoons) Salt (1 ½ teaspoons)

- Red pepper flakes, crushed (1/2 teaspoon)

- Allspice, ground (1/2 teaspoon)

- Bell pepper, yellow, sliced into half-inch portions (1 piece)

Yogurt sauce:

- Olive oil (2 tablespoons)

- Salt (1/4 teaspoon)

- Parsley, flat leaf, chopped finely (1 tablespoon)

- Yogurt, plain, Fat: free (1 cup)   Lemon juice, fresh (1 tablespoon)

- Garlic clove, chopped finely (1 piece)

Directions:

1. Mix the yogurt (1/2 cup), garlic cloves (4 pieces), olive oil (1 tablespoon), salt (1 teaspoon), lemon juice (2 tablespoons), pepper (1/4 teaspoon), allspice, cumin, and pepper flakes. Stir in the chicken and coat well. Cover and marinate in the fridge for two hours.

2. Preheat the air fryer at 400 degrees Fahrenheit.

3. Grease a rimmed baking sheet (18x13-inch) with cooking spray.

4. Toss the bell peppers and onion with remaining olive oil (2 tablespoons), pepper (1/4 teaspoon), and salt (1/2 teaspoon).

5. Arrange veggies on the baking sheet's left side and the marinated chicken thighs (drain first) on the right side. Cook in the air fryer for twenty-five to thirty minutes. Mix the yogurt sauce ingredients.

6. Slice air-fried chicken into half-inch strips.

7. Top each pita round with chicken strips, roasted veggies, cucumbers, and yogurt sauce.

***Nutrition*:**

- Calories: 381 kcal

- Fat: 10 g

- Carbs: 30 g

17. Easiest Tuna Cobbler Ever

Prep Time: 15 mins

Cook Time: 25 mins

Servings: 4

Ingredients:

- Water, cold (1/3 cup)

- Tuna, canned, drained (10 ounces)

- Sweet pickle relish (2 tablespoons)

- Mixed vegetables, frozen (1 ½ cups)

- Soup, cream of chicken, condensed (10 ¾ ounces) Pimientos, sliced, drained (2 ounces)

- Lemon juice (1 teaspoon) Paprika

Directions:

1. Preheat the air fryer at 375 degrees Fahrenheit.

2. Mist cooking spray into a round casserole (1 ½ quarts). Mix the frozen vegetables with milk, soup, lemon juice, relish, pimientos, and tuna in a saucepan.

3. Cook for 8 minutes over medium heat. Fill the casserole with the tuna mixture.

4. Mix the biscuit mix with cold water to form a soft dough. Beat for half a minute before dropping by four spoonfuls into the casserole.

5. Dust the dish with paprika before air-frying for twenty to twenty-five minutes.

Nutrition: Calories: 290 kcal ; Fat: 10 g ;Protein: 30g

CHAPTER 3

SALAD RECIPES

18.Broccoli with Herbs and Cheese

Prep Time: 7 mins

Cook Time: 15 mins

Servings: 4

Ingredients:

- 1/3 cup grated yellow cheese

- 1 large-sized head broccoli, stemmed and cut small florets

- 2 1/2 tablespoons canola oil

- 2 teaspoons dried rosemary

- 2 teaspoons dried basil

- Salt and ground black pepper, to taste

Directions:

1. Bring a medium pan filled with a lightly salted water to a boil.

2. Then, boil the broccoli florets for about 3 minutes. Then, drain the broccoli florets well; toss them with the canola oil, rosemary, basil, salt and black pepper.

3. Set your oven to 390 degrees F; arrange the seasoned broccoli in the cooking basket; set the timer for 17 minutes. Toss the broccoli halfway through the cooking process.

4. Serve warm topped with grated cheese and enjoy!

Nutrition:

- kcal: 112 g Carbohydrates: 3.8 g Protein: 8.3 g

- Fat: 2.2 g

19.Potato Carrot Salad

Prep Time: 15 mins

Cook Time: 10 mins

Servings: 1

Ingredients:

- Water

- One potato, sliced into cubes

- 1/2 carrots, cut into cubes

- 1/6 tablespoon milk

- 1/6 tablespoon Dijon mustard

- 1/24 cup mayonnaise

- Pepper to taste

- 1/3 teaspoons fresh thyme, chopped

- 1/6 stalk celery, chopped

- 1/6 scallions, chopped

- 1/6 slice turkey bacon, cooked crispy and crumbled

Directions:

1. Fill your pot with water.

2. Place it over medium-high heat.

3. Boil the potatoes and carrots for 10 to 12 minutes or until

   tender. Drain and let cool.

4. In a bowl, mix the milk mustard, mayo, pepper, and thyme.

5. Stir in the potatoes, carrots, and celery.

6. Coat evenly with the sauce.

7. Cover and refrigerate for 4 hours.

8. Top with the scallions and turkey bacon bits before serving.

Nutrition: kcal: 112 g; Carbohydrates: 3.8 g ; Protein: 8.3 g ;Fat: 2.2

g

20.Baked Cod & Vegetables

Prep Time: 20 mins

Cook Time: 15 mins

Servings: 4

Ingredients:

- 1 lb cod fillets
- 8 oz asparagus, chopped
- 3 cups broccoli, chopped
- ¼ cup parsley, minced
- ½ tsp lemon pepper seasoning
- ½ tsp paprika
- ¼ cup olive oil
- ¼ cup lemon juice
- 1 tsp salt

Directions:

1. Preheat oven to 400 F. Line a baking sheet with parchment paper and set aside.
2. In a small bowl, combine the lemon juice, paprika, olive oil, pepper spices, and salt.
3. Place the fish fillets in the center of the greaseproof paper. Arrange the broccoli and asparagus around the fish fillets.
4. Pour lemon juice mixture over the fish fillets and top with parsley.

5. Bake in preheated oven for 13-15 minutes.

6. Serve and enjoy.

Nutrition:

- kcal: 232 g Carbohydrates: 6.1 g Protein: 26 g

- Fat: 12 g

21.Squash Black Bean Bowl

Prep Time: 5 mins

Cook Time: 30 mins

Servings: 1

Ingredients:

- One large spaghetti squash, halved,

- 1/3 cup water (or 2 tbsp. olive oil, rubbed on the inside of squash)

- Black bean filling

- 1/2 15-oz can of black beans, emptied and rinsed

- 1/2 cup fire-roasted corn (or frozen sweet corn)

- 1/2 cup thinly sliced red cabbage

- 1/2 tbsp. chopped green onion, green and white parts

- 1/4 cup chopped fresh cilantro

- 1/2 lime, juiced or to taste

- Pepper and salt, to taste

  Avocado mash:

- One ripe avocado, mashed

- 1/2 lime, juiced or to taste

- 1/4 tsp. cumin

- Pepper and pinch of sea salt

Directions:

1. Preheat the oven to 400°F.

2. Chop the squash in part and scoop out the seeds with a spoon,

   like a pumpkin.

3. Fill the roasting pan with 1/3 cup of water. Lay the squash, cut

   side down, in the pan. Bake for 30 minutes until soft and

   tender.

4. While this is baking, mix all the ingredients for the black bean filling in a medium-sized bowl.

5. In a small dish, crush the avocado and blend in the ingredients for the avocado mash.

6. Eliminate the squash from the oven and let it cool for 5 minutes. Scrape the squash with a fork so that it looks like spaghetti noodles. Then, fill it with black bean filling and top with avocado mash.

7. Serve and enjoy.

Nutrition:

- kcal: 85 g

- Carbohydrates: 6.8 g

- Protein: 4.3 g

- Fat: 0.4 g

22.Fried Squash Croquettes

Prep Time: 5 mins

Cook Time: 18 mins

Servings: 4

Ingredients:

- 1/3 cup all-purpose flour

- 1/3 teaspoon freshly ground black pepper, or more to taste

- 1/3 teaspoon dried sage

- 4 cloves garlic, minced

- 1 ½ tablespoons olive oil

- 1/3 butternut squash, peeled and grated

- 2 eggs, well whisked

- 1 teaspoon fine sea salt

- A pinch of ground allspice

Directions:

1. Thoroughly combine all ingredients in a mixing bowl.

2. Preheat your Air Fryer to 345 degrees and set the timer for 17 minutes; cook until your fritters are browned; serve right away.

Nutrition:

- kcal: 132 g

- Carbohydrates: 9.1 g

- Protein: 5.6 g

- Fat: 10.3 g

23.Fried Avocado

Prep Time: 15 mins

Cook Time: 10 mins

Servings: 2

Ingredients:

- 2 avocados cut into wedges 25 mm. thick

- 50 g breadcrumbs

- 2 g garlic powder

- 2 g onion powder

- 1 g smoked paprika

- 1 g cayenne pepper

- Salt and pepper to taste

- 60 g all-purpose flour

- 2 eggs, beaten

- Nonstick spray oil

- Tomato sauce or ranch sauce, to serve

Directions:

1. Cut the avocados into 25 mm. thick pieces.

2. Combine the crumbs, garlic powder, onion powder, smoked

   paprika, cayenne pepper, and salt in a bowl.

3. Separate each wedge of avocado in the flour, then dip the

   beaten eggs and stir in the breadcrumb mixture.

4. Preheat the air fryer.

5. Place the avocados in the preheated air fryer baskets, spray with

   oil spray, and cook at 205°C for 10 minutes. Turn the fried

   avocado halfway through cooking and sprinkle with cooking oil.

6. Serve with tomato sauce or ranch sauce.

Nutrition: kcal: 122 g; Carbohydrates: 1.9 g; Protein: 4.6 g ; Fat: 8 g

24. Garlic Chive Cauliflower Mash

Prep Time: 25 mins

Cook Time: 14 mins

Servings: 6

Ingredients:

- 4 cups cauliflower

- 1/3 cup vegetarian mayonnaise

- 1 garlic clove

- 1/2 teaspoon. kosher salt

- 1 tablespoon. water

- 1/8 teaspoon. pepper

- 1/4 teaspoon. lemon juice

- 1/2 teaspoon lemon zest

- 1 tablespoon Chives, minced

Directions:

1. In a bowl that is save to microwave, add the cauliflower, mayo, garlic, water, and salt/pepper and mix until the cauliflower is well coated. Cook on high for 15-18 minutes, until the cauliflower is almost mushy.

2. Blend the mixture in a strong blender until completely smooth, adding a little more water if the mixture is too chunky. Season with the remaining ingredients and serve.

Nutrition:

- kcal: 162 g

- Carbohydrates: 14.1 g

- Protein: 2.6 g

- Fat: 18 g

25.Grilled Eggplants

Prep Time: 15 mins

Cook Time: 10 mins

Servings: 4

Ingredients:

- 1 large eggplant, cut into thick circles

- Salt and pepper to taste

- 1 tsp. smoked paprika

- 1 tbsp. coconut flour

- 1 tsp. lime juice

- 1 tbsp. olive oil

Directions:

1. Coat the eggplants in smoked paprika, salt, pepper, lime juice, coconut flour, and let it sit for 10 minutes.

2. In a grilling pan, add the olive oil.

3. Grill the eggplants for 3 minutes on each side.

4. Serve.

Nutrition:

- kcal: 235 g

- Carbohydrates: 4.2 g

- Protein: 0.8 g

- Fat: 0.3 g

CHAPTER 4

SNACKS AND APPETIZER RECIPES

26. Tasty WW Pancakes

Prep Time: 12 mins

Cook Time: 10 mins

Servings: 4

Ingredients:

- 4 large eggs, organic

- Salt and black pepper, to taste

Directions:

1. Place the eggs into the air fryer basket.

2. AIR Fry them for 8-10 minutes at 300 degrees F

3. remove the eggs and transfer them to very cold water. Peel,

slice and serve with a sprinkle of salt and black pepper.

Serving Suggestion: Serve with roasted nuts

Variation Tip: Use paprika instead of black pepper

Nutrition:

- Calories: 74 kcal ;

- Fat: 4 g ;

- Carbs: 0.3 g;

- Protein: 6 g

27.Garlic Mushrooms

Prep Time: 10 mins

Cook Time: 15 mins

Servings: 3

Ingredients:

- 10 ounces of mushrooms, washed and dried
- 1 teaspoon olive oil
- ½ teaspoon garlic powder
- 1 teaspoon Worcestershire sauce
- 1 tablespoon parsley, chopped
- Salt and black pepper, to taste
- 1 teaspoon of lemon juice

Directions:

1. Cut the washed mushrooms in half.
2. Add it to the bowl and mix in olive oil, salt, garlic powder, black pepper, Worcestershire sauce, parsley, and toss well.
3. Add mushrooms to a bowl then toss.
4. Put it into air fryer basket and air fry at 375 for 15 minutes.
5. Remember to toss and shake halfway through,
6. Once cooked, squeeze lemon and top with chopped parsley.

Serving Suggestion: Serve it with mashed potatoes **Variation Tip:** Use vegetable oil instead of olive oil.

Nutrition:

- Calories: 30 kcal

- Fat: 3 g

- Carbs: 4 g

- Protein: 3 g

28.Sticky Chicken Thai Wings

Prep Time: 10 mins

Cook Time: 30 mins

Servings: 6

Ingredients:

- 3 pounds chicken wings removed
- 1 tsp sea salt to taste

For the glaze:

- ¾ cup Thai sweet chili sauce
- ¼ cup soy sauce
- 4 tsp brown sugar
- 4 tsp rice wine vinegar
- 3 tsp fish sauce
- 2 tsp lime juice
- 1 tsp lemon grass minced
- 2 tsp sesame oil
- 1 tsp garlic minced

Directions:

1. Preheat the oven to 350 degrees Fahrenheit. Lightly spray your baking tray with cooking tray and set it aside. To prepare the glaze combine the ingredients in a small bowl and whisk them until they are well combined. Pour half of the mixture into a pan and reserve the rest.

2. Trim any excess skin off the wing edges and season it with pepper and salt. Add the wings to a baking tray and pour the sauce over the wings tossing them for the sauce to evenly coat. Arrange them in a single layer and bake them for 15 minutes.

3. While the wings are in the oven, bring your glaze to simmer in medium heat until there are visible bubbles. Once the wings are cooled on one side rotate each piece and bake for an extra 10 minutes. Baste them and return them into the oven to allow for more cooking until they are golden brown. Garnish with onion slices, cilantro, chili flakes and sprinkle the remain salt. Serving with glaze of your choice.

Nutrition:

- Calories: 250 kcal
- Fat: 16 g
- Carbs: 19 g
- Protein: 20g

29.Roasted Air Fry Nuts

Prep Time: 10 mins

Cook Time: 8 mins

Servings: 5

Ingredients:

- 1 cup almonds

- 1 cup peanuts

- Pinch of sea salt

Directions:

1. Preheat the air fryer at 300 degrees F.

2. toss the nuts with sea salt Put the nuts in an air fryer basket

   and set the timer to 8 minutes at 325 degrees F.

3. To toss the nuts halfway through

4. Cool the nuts before serving.

Serving Suggestion: Serve as a delicious snack along with fresh

fruits

Variation Tip: Use any other nuts that you personally like.

Nutrition:

- Calories: 334 kcal

- Fat: 25 g

- Carbs: 10 g

- Protein: 15 g

30.Cheesy Mashed Sweet Potato Cakes

Prep Time: 10 mins

Cook Time: 30 mins **Servings**: 4

Ingredients:

- ¾ cup bread crumbs

- 4 cups mashed potatoes ½ cup onions

- 2 cup of grated mozzarella cheese

- ¼ cup fresh grated parmesan cheese

- 2 large cloves finely chopped   1 egg

- 2 tsp finely chopped parsley Salt and pepper to taste

Directions:

1. Line your baking sheet with foil. Wash, peel and cut the sweet

potatoes into 6 pieces. Arrange them inside the baking sheet and

drizzle a small amount of oil on top before seasoning with salt and pepper.

2. Cover with a baking sheet and bake it for 45 minutes. once cooked transfer them into a mixing bowl and mash them well with a potato masher. To the sweet potatoes in a bowl add green onions, parmesan, mozzarella, garlic, egg, parsley and bread crumbs. Mash and combine the mixture together using the masher.

3. Put the remaining ¼ cup of the breadcrumbs in a place. Scoop a tsp of mixture into your palm and form round patties around ½ and inch thick. Dredge your patties in the breadcrumbs to cover both sides and set them aside. Heat a tablespoon of oil in a medium nonstick pan. when the oil is hot begin to cook the patties

4. in batches 4 or 5 per session and cook each side for 6 minutes

until they turn golden brown. Using a spoon or spatula flip them.

Add oil to prevent burning.

__Nutrition__:

- Calories: 120 kcal

- Fat: 6 g

- Carbs: 15 g

- Protein: 5 g

31.Coconut Fudge

Prep Time: 20 mins

Cook Time: 60 mins

Servings: 12

Ingredients:

- 2 cups coconut oil

- ½ cup dark cocoa powder

- ½ cup coconut cream

- ¼ cup almonds, chopped ¼ cup coconut, shredded

- 1 teaspoon almond extract   Pinch of salt   Stevia to taste

Directions:

1. Pour your coconut oil and coconut cream in a bowl, whisking with an electric beater until smooth. Once the mixture becomes smooth and glossy, do not continue.

2. Begin to add in your cocoa powder while mixing slowly, making sure that there aren't any lumps.

3. Add in the rest of your ingredients, and mix well. Line a pan with parchment paper, and freeze until it sets. Slice into squares before serving.

Nutrition:

- Calories: 176 kcal

- Fat: 20g

- Carbs: 4 g

- Protein: 3 g

32.Fluffy Bites

Prep Time: 20 mins

Cook Time: 60 mins

Servings: 6

Ingredients:

- 1 teaspoons cinnamon

- 1/3 cup sour cream

- 1 cups heavy cream

- 1/2 teaspoon scraped vanilla bean

- ¼ teaspoon cardamom

- 2 egg yolks

- Stevia to taste

Directions:

1. Start by whisking your egg yolks until creamy and smooth.

2. Get out a double boiler, and add your eggs with the rest of your ingredients. Mix well.   Remove from heat, allowing it to cool until it reaches room temperature.

3. Refrigerate for an hour before whisking well.

4. Pour into molds, and freeze for at least an hour before serving.

Nutrition:

- Calories: 366 kcal

- Fat: 35 g

- Carbs: 6 g

- Protein: 8 g

33. Easy Vanilla Bombs

Prep Time: 20 mins

Cook Time: 45 mins

Servings: 7

Ingredients:

- 1/2 cup macadamia nuts, unsalted

- ¼ cup coconut oil

- ¼ cup butter

- 1 teaspoons vanilla extract, sugar-free

- 10 drops liquid Stevia

- 1 tablespoons erythritol, powdered

Directions:

1. Pulse your macadamia nuts in a blender, and then combine all

   of your ingredients together. Mix well.

2. Get out mini muffin tins with a tablespoon and a half of the

   mixture.

3. Refrigerate it for a half hour before serving.

Nutrition:

- Calories: 125 kcal

- Fat: 5 g

- Carbs: 6 g

- Protein: 1 g

34.Grandma's Rice

Prep Time: 15 mins

Cook Time: 2 h

Servings: 4

Ingredients:

- 40 g butter

- 1/2 cup brown sugar

- 1/2 cup arborio rice

- 3 cups milk

- 1/2 tbsp. ground cinnamon

- 1/8 tbsp. ground nutmeg

- 1 tbsp. vanilla paste

- 1/2 cup raisins

- 300 ml. cream

Directions:

1. Preheat oven to 300F. Grease a 1-liter ability oven-safe plate.

2. Heat butter in a saucepan and add sugar and rice.

3. Stir for 1 minute to thoroughly coat the rice. Remove from heat

and wish in milk, spices, and vanilla.

4. Stir through raisins then pour into prepared dish.

5. Bake for 30 minutes, then remove from the oven and stir well.

6. Drizzle over the cream and return to the oven for an additional

hour.

7. Check that the rice is cooked through.

8. Return to the oven for 15-30 minutes if required.

9. Serve with extra cream and nutmeg.

Nutrition:

- Calories: 200 kcal Fat: 20 g Carbs: 26 g Protein: 28 g

CHAPTER 5

DINNER RECIPES

35.Pork and Peppers Chili

Preparation Time: 6 minutes **Cooking Time:** 8 hours 5 min

Servings: 4

Ingredients:

- 1 red onion, chopped   2 pounds' pork, ground

- 4 garlic cloves, minced   2 red bell peppers, chopped

- 1 celery stalk, chopped   25 ounces' fresh tomatoes, peeled,

  crushed   ¼ cup green chilies, chopped

- 2 tablespoons fresh oregano, chopped

- 2 tablespoons chili powder

- A pinch of salt and black pepper

- A drizzle of olive oil

Directions:

1. Heat up a sauté pan with the oil over medium-high heat and add the onion, garlic and the meat. Mix and brown for 5 minutes then transfer to your slow cooker.

2. Add the rest of the ingredients, toss, cover and cook on low for 8 hours.

3. Divide everything into bowls and serve.

Nutrition:

- Calories: 440 Fat: 12 Fiber 6.4

- Carbs 20

- Protein 62

36.Greek Style Quesadillas

Preparation Time: 12 minutes

Cooking Time: 10 minutes **Servings:** 4

Ingredients:

- 4 whole wheat tortillas

- 1 cup Mozzarella cheese, shredded

- 1 cup fresh spinach, chopped

- 2 tablespoon Greek yogurt

- 1 egg, beaten ¼ cup green olives, sliced

- 1 tablespoon olive oil

- 1/3 cup fresh cilantro, chopped

Directions:

- In the bowl, combine together Mozzarella cheese, spinach, yogurt, egg, olives, and cilantro.

- Then pour olive oil in the skillet.

- Place one tortilla in the skillet and spread it with Mozzarella mixture.

- Top it with the second tortilla and spread it with cheese mixture again.

- Then place the third tortilla and spread it with all remaining cheese mixture.

- Cover it with the last tortilla and fry it for 5 minutes from each side over the medium heat.

Nutrition:

- Calories: 191 Fat: 7.2

- Fiber 3

- Carbs 23.4

- Protein 8.2

37.Creamy Penne

Preparation Time: 12 min

Cooking Time: 25 min

Servings: 4

Ingredients:

- ½ cup penne, dried

- 9 oz. chicken fillet

- 1 teaspoon Italian seasoning

- 1 tablespoon olive oil

- 1 tomato, chopped

- 1 cup heavy cream

- 1 tablespoon fresh basil, chopped

- ½ teaspoon salt

- 2 oz. Parmesan, grated

- 1 cup water, for cooking

Directions:

1. Pour water in the pan, add penne, and boil it for 15 minutes.

   Then drain water.

2. Pour olive oil in the skillet and heat it up.

3. Slice the chicken fillet and put it in the hot oil.

4. Sprinkle chicken with Italian seasoning and roast for 2 minutes

   from each side.

5. Then add fresh basil, salt, tomato, and grated cheese.

6. Stir well.

7. Add heavy cream and cooked penne.

8. Cook the meal for 5 minutes

Nutrition:

- Calories: 385 Fat: 23.2 Fiber 0.1 Carbs 17.3 Protein 17.5

38.Instant Pot Chipotle Chicken & Cauliflower

Rice Bowls

Preparation Time: 12min **Cooking Time:** 20 min **Servings:** 4

Ingredients:

- 1/3 cup of salsa   1 quantity of 14.5 oz. of can fire-roasted diced

  tomatoes   1 canned chipotle pepper + 1 teaspoon sauce

- ½ teaspoon of dried oregano   1 teaspoon of cumin

- 1 ½ lb. of boneless, skinless chicken breast

- ¼ teaspoon of salt   1 cup of reduced-fat shredded Mexican

  cheese blend   4 cups of frozen riced cauliflower

- ½ medium-sized avocado, sliced

Directions:

1. Combine the first ingredients in a blender and blend until they

become smooth

2. Place chicken inside your instant pot, and pour the sauce over it.

Cover the lid and close the pressure valve.

3. Set it to 20 minutes at high temperature. Let the pressure

release on its own before opening.

4. Remove the piece and the chicken and then add it back to the

sauce.

5. Microwave the riced cauliflower according to the directions on

the package.

6. Before you serve, divide the riced cauliflower, cheese, avocado,

and chicken equally among the four bowls.

Nutrition:

- Calories: 285 Protein: 34 g

- Carbohydrate: 18 g

- Fat: 11 g

39.Homemade Chicken Broth

Preparation Time: 6 minutes **Cooking Time**: 30 minutes **Servings**: 4

Ingredients:

- 1 tablespoon olive oil

- 1 chopped onion

- 2 chopped stalks celery

- 2 chopped carrots

- 1 whole chicken

- 2+ quarts of water

- 1 tablespoon salt

- ½ teaspoon pepper

- 1 teaspoon fresh sage

Directions:

1. Sauté vegetables in oil.

2. Add chicken and water and simmer for 2+ hours until the chicken falls off the bone. Keep adding water as needed.

3. Remove the chicken carcass from the broth, place on a platter, and let it cool. Pull chicken off the carcass and put it into the broth.

4. Pour broth mixture into pint and quart mason jars. Be sure to add meat to each jar.

5. Leave one full inch of space from the top of the jar or it will crack when it freezes as liquids expand. Place jars in freezer for up to a year.

6. Take out and use whenever you make a soup.

Nutrition:

- Calories: 210 Fat: 6g Carbs: 15g

- Protein: 21g

40.Grilled Salmon with Pineapple Salsa

Prep Time: 6 Minutes

Cook Time: 30 Minutes **Servings:** 4

Ingredients

- 4 salmon fillets

- Salt and pepper to taste

- 2 tablespoons Cajun seasoning

- 1 fresh pineapple, peeled and diced

- 1 cup cherry tomatoes, quartered

- 2 tablespoons chopped cilantro

- 2 tablespoons chopped parsley

- 1 teaspoon dried mint

- 2 tablespoons lemon juice

- 2 tablespoons extra virgin olive oil

- 1 teaspoon honey

- Salt and pepper to taste

Directions:

1. Add salt, pepper and Cajun seasoning to the fish.

2. Heat a grill pan over medium flame. Cook fish on the grill on each

side for 3-4 minutes.

3. For the salsa, mix the pineapple, tomatoes, cilantro, parsley,

mint, lemon juice and honey in a bowl. Season with salt and

pepper.

4. Serve the grilled salmon with the pineapple salsa.

Nutrition:

- Calories 330

- Fat 11g Carbs 7

- Protein 33

41.Fish Stew

Preparation Time: 6 minutes **Cooking Time**: 30 minutes **Servings:** 4

Ingredients:

- 1 tablespoon olive oil

- 1 chopped onion or leek

- 2 chopped stalks celery

- 2 chopped carrots

- 1 clove minced garlic

- 1 tablespoon parsley

- 1 bay leaf

- 1 clove

- 1/8 teaspoon kelp or dulse (seaweed)

- ¼ teaspoon salt

- Fish—leftover, cooked, diced

- 2–3 cups chicken or vegetable broth

Directions:

1. Add all of ingredients and simmer on the stove for 20 minutes.

Nutrition:

- Calories: 340

- Fat: 14g

- Fiber: 10g

- Carbs: 8g

- Protein: 10g

42.Prosciutto Spinach Salad

Preparation Time: 7 minutes

Cooking Time: 5 minutes **Servings**: 2

Ingredients:

- 2 cups baby spinach

- 1/3 lb. prosciutto

- 1 cantaloupe

- 1 avocado

- ¼ cup diced red onion handful of raw, unsalted walnuts

Directions:

1. Put a cup of spinach on each plate.

2. Top with the diced prosciutto, cubes of balls of melon, slices of

   avocado, a handful of red onion and a few walnuts.

3. Add some freshly ground pepper, if you like.

4. Serve!

Nutrition:

- Calories: 346

- Carbs: 10 g

- Fat: 8 g

- Protein: 25 g

- Fiber: 20 g

CHAPTER 6

DESSERT RECIPES

---

43. Mandarin Cream

Preparation Time: 22 mins **Cook Time**: 0 minutes **Servings:** 8

Ingredients:

- 2 mandarins, peeled and cut into segments

- Juice of 2 mandarins   2 tablespoons stevia

- 4 eggs, whisked   ¾ cup stevia

- ¾ cup almonds, ground

Directions:

1. In a blender, combine the mandarins with the mandarin's juice and the other ingredients, whisk well, divide into cups

and keep in the fridge for 20 minutes before serving.

***Nutrition*:**

- Calories: 105

- Fat: 3.4

- Fiber 0

- Carbs 2.2

- Protein 4.2

44. Creamy Mint Strawberry Mix

Preparation Time: 12 mins

Cooking Time: 30 mins **Servings:** 6

Ingredients:

- Cooking spray

- ¼ cup stevia

- 1 and ½ cup almond flour

- 1 teaspoon baking powder

- 1 cup almond milk

- 1 egg, whisked

- 2 cups strawberries, sliced

- 1 tablespoon mint, chopped

- 1 teaspoon lime zest, grated

- ½ cup whipping cream

Directions:

1. In a bowl, combine the almond with the strawberries, mint and

   the other ingredients except the cooking spray and whisk well.

2. Grease 6 ramekins with the cooking spray, pour the strawberry

   mix inside, introduce in the oven and bake at 350 degrees F for

   30 minutes.

3. Cool down and serve

Nutrition:

- Calories: 197

- Fat: 6.2

- Fiber 2.2

- Carbs 6.3

- Protein 8.1

45. Vanilla Cake

Preparation Time: 10 min

Cooking Time: 25 min **Servings:** 5

Ingredients:

- 1 ½ cups almond flour

- 1 ½ teaspoons baking powder

- ½cup olive oil

- ½ and ½ cup almond milk

- 1 cup stevia

- 1 cups water

- ½ tablespoon lime juice

- 1 teaspoons vanilla extract

- Cooking spray

Directions:

1. In a bowl, mix the almond flour with the baking powder, the oil

   and the rest of the ingredients except the cooking spray and

   whisk well.

2. Pour the mix into a cake pan greased with the cooking spray,

   introduce in the oven and bake at 370 degrees F for 25

   minutes.

3. Leave the cake to cool down, cut and serve!

Nutrition:

- Calories: 100

- Fat: 3.8

- Fiber 1.3

- Carbs 2.7

- Protein 2.2

46.Pumpkin Cream

Preparation Time: 5 minutes **Cook Time:** 5 minutes **Servings: 2**

Ingredients:

- 2 cups canned pumpkin flesh

- 2 tablespoons stevia

- 1 teaspoon vanilla extract

- 2 tablespoons water

- A pinch of pumpkin spice

Directions:

1. In a pan, combine the pumpkin flesh with the other ingredients, simmer for 5 minutes, divide into cups and serve cold.

Nutrition:

- Calories: 190 Fat: 3.2 Fiber 4.3 Carbs 7.4

- Protein 3.2

47.Chia and Berries Smoothie Bowl

Preparation Time: 5 minutes **Cooking Time:** 0 minutes **Servings: 2**

Ingredients:

- 1 and ½ cup almond milk   1 cup blackberries

- ¼ cup strawberries, chopped   1 and ½ tablespoons chia

  seeds   1 teaspoon cinnamon powder

Directions:

1. In a blender, combine the blackberries with the strawberries

   and the rest of the ingredients, pulse well, divide into small

   bowls and serve cold.

Nutrition:

- Calories: 180 Fat: 3.2 Fiber 3.3 Carbs 8.2

- Protein 3.1

48.Minty Coconut Cream

Preparation Time: 4 minutes

Cooking Time: 0 minutes **Servings:** 2

Ingredients:

- 1 banana, peeled   2 cups coconut flesh, shredded

- 3 tablespoons mint, chopped   1 and ½ cups coconut water

- 2 tablespoons stevia   ½ avocado, pitted and peeled

Directions:

1. In a blender, combine the coconut with the banana and the rest

   of the ingredients, pulse well, divide into cups and serve cold.

Nutrition:

- Calories: 191 Fat: 5.2 Fiber 3.3

- Carbs 7.4

- Protein 3.2

49.Grapes Stew

Preparation: 10 min **Cooking**: 10 min **Servings**: 4

Ingredients:

- 2/3 cup stevia   1 tablespoon olive oil 1/3 cup coconut water

- 1 teaspoon vanilla extract 1 teaspoon lemon zest, grated

- 2 cup red grapes, halved

Directions:

1. Heat up a pan with the water over medium heat, add the oil, stevia and the rest of the ingredients, toss, simmer for 10 minutes, divide into cups and serve.

Nutrition:

- Calories: 120 Fat: 3.5 Fiber 1.2

- Carbs 2.3

- Protein 0.5

50. Apple Couscous Pudding

Preparation Time: 10 min **Cooking Time**: 25 min **Servings:** 4

Ingredients:

- ½ cup couscous 1 and ½ cups milk   ¼ cup apple, cored and

  chopped   3 tablespoons stevia   ½ teaspoon rose water

- 1 tablespoon orange zest, grated

Directions:

1. Heat up a pan with the milk over medium heat,

2. add the couscous and the rest of the ingredients, whisk, simmer

   for 25 minutes, divide into bowls and serve.

Nutrition:

- Calories: 152 Fat: 4.2 Fiber 5.5

- Carbs 7.3 Protein 4.2

Conclusion

With regards to food, I have learned to see food as the major source of energy that powers my body and to find profound fulfillment in eating things that are nutritious. The Lean and Green diet cookbook is a healthy and tasty approach to eating healthy and losing weight while also enjoying your favorite foods. There is no reward better than the satisfaction you derive from making the right choices. Kick out the old emotional eating habits of using food as a reward and embrace a new healthier eating habit with this Lean and Green diet cookbook.